Fish Migration

by Jen Breach

T0015133

FOCUS
READERS.

BEACON

www.focusreaders.com

Focus Readers is distributed by North Star Editions:
sales@northstareditions.com | 888-417-0195

Produced for Focus Readers by Red Line Editorial.

Photographs ©: Shutterstock Images, cover, 1, 4, 14, 17, 19, 22, 27, 29; iStockphoto, 7, 8, 11, 13, 25; Andrew J. Martinez/Science Source, 20–21

Library of Congress Cataloging-in-Publication Data
Names: Breach, Jen, author.
Title: Fish migration / by Jen Breach.
Description: Lake Elmo, MN : Focus Readers, [2024] | Series: Animal migrations | Includes bibliographical references and index. | Audience: Grades 2-3
Identifiers: LCCN 2023005792 (print) | LCCN 2023005793 (ebook) | ISBN 9781637396070 (hardcover) | ISBN 9781637396643 (paperback) | ISBN 9781637397756 (pdf) | ISBN 9781637397213 (ebook)
Subjects: LCSH: Fishes--Migration--Juvenile literature.
Classification: LCC QL617.2 .B73 2024 (print) | LCC QL617.2 (ebook) | DDC 591.56/8--dc23/eng/20230322
LC record available at https://lccn.loc.gov/2023005792
LC ebook record available at https://lccn.loc.gov/2023005793

Printed in the United States of America
Mankato, MN
082023

About the Author

In 2012, Jen Breach (they/them) migrated 10,371 miles (16,700 km) from Melbourne, Australia, to New York City. Jen has worked as a bagel-baker, a code-breaker, a ticket-taker, and a trouble-maker. They now work as a writer, the best job ever, in Philadelphia, Pennsylvania.

Table of Contents

Chapter 1

A Long Swim

A female blue shark swims through the water. She is traveling east across the Atlantic Ocean. She rides the **currents**. In a few months, she reaches the coast of Africa. The shark stops and gives birth.

 Blue sharks grow to lengths of approximately 10 feet (3 m).

But her journey is not over. When spring comes, it is time for **mating**. So, the blue shark heads west. She crosses the ocean again. She reaches the coast of North America. In these waters, the shark finds a mate.

Migrating blue sharks swim up to 9,500 miles (15,000 km). It is

Fun Fact

Blue sharks follow a clockwise path around the Atlantic Ocean.

 Blue sharks can give birth to more than 100 babies at a time.

the longest fish migration in the world. When the journey is done, they don't stay put for long. They will repeat the migration in a year or two.

Chapter 2

Why Migrate?

Many fish stay in one area for their whole lives. But other **species** migrate. Some fish migrate to find food. Others migrate to lay eggs.

Fish often use ocean currents to migrate. Flounder are one example.

 An adult flounder has both of its eyes on the same side of its head.

Each year, flounder release their eggs in the Gulf of Mexico. Then they move to feeding areas. These areas are farther from land. Currents help the flounder move without much effort. Their flat bodies can float easily.

Sometimes flounder don't want to move on a current. So, they bury themselves in the sand. They wait until the currents shift back again.

Sardines swim from one ocean to another. They begin in the Atlantic

 A group of sardines can include millions of fish.

Ocean. But a cold current forms off the southern coast of Africa. This current moves the sardines up Africa's east coast. They swim into the Indian Ocean.

Small fish such as sardines usually swim together. These huge groups are called schools. A school of sardines can be 4 miles (7 km) long.

When sardines migrate, **predators** follow. These include sharks, whales, and birds. The

Tuna migrate using Earth's **magnetic field**. These fish can tell north from south.

 A shark feeds on sardines off the coast of Africa.

predators eat many of the sardines. But migrating together helps more of the sardines survive.

Chapter 3

Salt Water to Fresh Water

Some fish migrate between salt water and fresh water. Adult salmon do this to **spawn**. They start in oceans, which are salt water. Then they swim to freshwater rivers. There, they travel upstream.

 People build fish ladders to help salmon swim around dams.

The salmon fight strong currents for days or weeks. Many salmon do not survive.

The salmon are trying to reach their birthplace. When salmon are young, they learn the river's smell. Months later, it is time to spawn. The salmon might be very far away. But they remember the

Fun Fact

Salmon migration is an important part of many **ecosystems.**

▷ **Sockeye salmon turn red when they return to their spawning grounds.**

smell of their home river. They do not stop traveling until they find it. Salmon can swim more than 2,000 miles (3,200 km) to reach their destination.

Herring also migrate from salt water to fresh water. Like salmon, they must go upstream. But salmon make this trip only once. Herring go between the river and the sea several times in their lives. Bass make the journey many times as well. They head toward deep water in the summer. In the fall, they head back upstream.

Some fish, including most eels, take the opposite journey. They are born in freshwater areas.

Largemouth bass can live for more than 15 years in the wild.

They spend most of their lives there. Then, when it is time to mate, they migrate downstream. After spawning once in the ocean, they die.

Eel Migration

Many eels live in oceans. But American eels spawn in the Atlantic Ocean and then move to fresh water. First, the eel eggs float in the ocean. After hatching, baby eels drift on currents. They travel up to 5,000 miles (8,000 km). In time, they reach fresh water. Then they wriggle upstream. They make homes in lakes and rivers.

When the eels are grown, they migrate back to the ocean. They lay their eggs there. After that, they die. But the life cycle continues.

American eels hunt at night and rest during the day.

Chapter 4

Migration in Fresh Water

Some fish move between different areas of fresh water. In Cambodia, **monsoons** happen during the wet season. Storms flood the Mekong River. The water flows into a lake called Tonle Sap.

 Houses along Tonle Sap are built on tall stilts.

More than five billion fish migrate with the floodwaters. They include Mekong giant catfish and striped tiger perch. Freshwater pufferfish also make the journey. So do mud eels and money fish. It is one of the biggest animal migrations on Earth.

Six months later, it is the dry season. The rain stops. The Mekong's water level drops. Water flows back out of Tonle Sap. That causes fish to flow from the lake back to the river. Along the

> The Mekong giant catfish can weigh 600 pounds (270 kg).

way, people catch many of the fish for food. But the rest swim far away. They go back to their breeding grounds.

Some carp move up and down rivers. They might travel hundreds of miles. But other carp stay in the same lakes all year. During winter, they gather in the warmer areas. When it is spring, they swim across the lake. They move to better breeding areas.

Fun Fact

Hawaiian freshwater goby migrate up waterfalls. They use their mouths and fins as suction cups.

 Carp tend to stay near the bottom of lakes and rivers.

FOCUS ON
Fish Migration

Write your answers on a separate piece of paper.

1. Write a paragraph describing the main idea of Chapter 2.

2. Which type of fish migration do you find most interesting? Why?

3. What is one kind of fish that migrates between the Mekong River and Tonle Sap each year?
    A. striped tiger perch
    B. American eel
    C. flounder

4. What is most likely to make an area good for spawning?
    A. The water is very hot.
    B. The water does not have any food.
    C. The water has few predators.

5. What does **destination** mean in this book?

They do not stop traveling until they find it. Salmon can swim more than 2,000 miles (3,200 km) to reach their destination.

    A. a place where an animal is trying to go
    B. a place where an animal begins its trip
    C. a place where fish cannot survive

6. What does the word **drift** mean in this book?

First, the eel eggs float in the ocean. After hatching, baby eels drift on currents.

    A. mate and release eggs
    B. move slowly on the water
    C. stay in the same place

Answer key on page 32.

Glossary

currents
Water movements that go in a certain direction.

ecosystems
Communities of living things and how they interact with their surrounding environments.

magnetic field
The space around an object (such as a moon or planet) in which its magnetic force can be detected.

mating
Coming together in order to have babies.

migrating
Moving from one region to another.

monsoons
Strong winds that cause extreme wet and dry seasons in an area.

predators
Animals that hunt other animals for food.

spawn
To release eggs.

species
Groups of animals or plants that are alike and can breed with one another.

To Learn More

BOOKS

Gieseke, Tyler. *Migration Cycles*. Minneapolis: Lerner Publications, 2023.

Pembroke, Ethan. *The Shark Encyclopedia*. Minneapolis: Abdo Publishing, 2021.

Schuetz, Kari. *Salmon Migration*. Minneapolis: Bellwether Media, 2019.

NOTE TO EDUCATORS

Visit **www.focusreaders.com** to find lesson plans, activities, links, and other resources related to this title.

Index

A
Atlantic Ocean, 5–6, 10–11, 20

B
bass, 18
blue sharks, 5–7

C
carp, 26
currents, 5, 9–11, 16, 20

E
eels, 18–19, 20, 24

F
flounder, 9–10

G
Gulf of Mexico, 10

H
herring, 18

I
Indian Ocean, 11

M
magnetic fields, 12
Mekong River, 23–24

P
predators, 12–13

S
salmon, 15–18
sardines, 10–13
spawning, 15–16, 19, 20

T
Tonle Sap, 23–24